Safety Tips

real kids/real science books contain lots of ideas and suggestions for observing and collecting animals and plants in woods, fields, ponds, drainage ditches, and at the shore.
If you follow a few simple rules, your adventures will be safe and enjoyable.

▶ Plan your field trips with your parents or guardian, even if you are going to collect or observe in a familiar place. Make sure they are aware if you need to venture into even shallow water.

▶ Wear appropriate dress. Protect your feet when wading; protect your arms and legs in heavy underbrush.

▶ Share your adventures with a friend.

Happy
Birthday,
Kaylyn!
Love, Mom & Dad
7/6/97, Canada

Woods, Ponds, & Fields

"Study nature, not books." —LOUIS AGASSIZ

Woods, Ponds, & Fields

written by Ellen Doris
original photography by Len Rubenstein

PRODUCED IN ASSOCIATION WITH
The Children's School of Science
Woods Hole, Massachusetts

T&H THAMES AND HUDSON

What is this book about?

his book will help you explore the unique relationships between certain plants and animals and the living and non-living things that share their environment. You will find lots of projects, field trips, ideas, and suggestions for exploring the ecology of woods, ponds, and fields.

How to use this book

Woods, Ponds, and Fields is organized as a collection of separate projects, investigations, and discoveries. It shows you where to look for common plants and animals, and how to study them in the context of their natural environment. You don't have to follow the book step by step from beginning to end. We suggest you browse through it first. Look for a field trip that's easy to do near your home, like birdwatching—even city parks are home to many kinds of birds. This book will be a lot more fun if you share some of the projects and field trips with someone else, a friend or a parent. Remember to be a safe scientist—always plan your trips with an adult.

Where can you get specimens and subjects to study? And equipment?

First of all, try to collect specimens yourself. And, except for a hand lens and binoculars, you shouldn't need much equipment to explore woods, ponds, and fields. There is a list of specimens and equipment on page 62 that can be ordered from biological supply houses. But don't feel you have to order all of it at once. You'll be surprised at how many kitchen and household items can be adapted to your needs. You can probably borrow expensive items, like microscopes and binoculars, from your school or a local nature center.

What is a conifer? And how do you pronounce Carduelis tristus?

Check out the glossary on page 63, which defines all the terms that are printed in **bold** type. But don't get bogged down trying to pronounce long Latin names; sound them out as well as you can and go on.

Think for yourself

You'll probably have to adapt some of the projects you find in this book. Remember, not every project or field trip goes according to plan. For instance, you may not find woodland animals no matter how hard you try. Has a recent rain washed away tell-tale traces? Have you looked in, on, and under things? Think about what may have gone wrong, and try again.

The Children's School of Science
Woods Hole, Massachusetts

Each summer, in an old-fashioned school-house whose rooms are crowded with plants, nets, microscopes, and bubbling aquaria, several hundred children between the ages of seven and sixteen attend classes for two hours each morning. Led by teachers who are experts in their field, the children take frequent field trips and work with each other on projects and experiments. The classes are informal, and courses range from Seashore Exploration to Ornithology to Neurobiology. For over seventy-five years, this remarkable institution has fostered the joy of discovery by encouraging direct observation of natural phenomena.

Contents

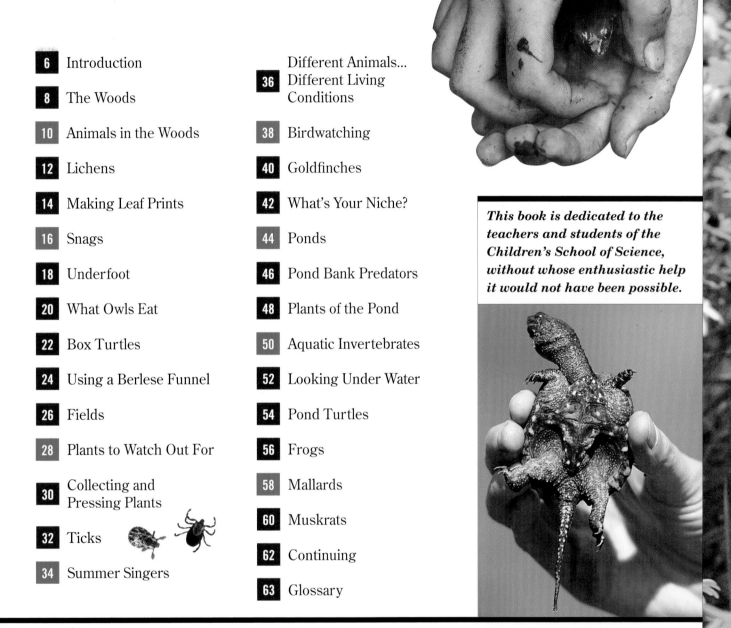

This book is dedicated to the teachers and students of the Children's School of Science, without whose enthusiastic help it would not have been possible.

Copyright © 1994 Thames and Hudson Inc., New York
First published in the United States in 1994 by Thames and Hudson Inc., 500 Fifth Avenue, New York, New York 10110

Photos copyright © Len Rubenstein unless otherwise indicated.

Library of Congress Catalog Card Number 93-61889

Design, typesetting, and pre-press production by Beth Tondreau Design ■ Managing Editor, Laurance Rosenzweig

Color separations made by The Sarabande Press ■ Printed and bound in Hong Kong

Introduction

Some scientists are interested in the relationships between different kinds of plants and animals, as well as the connections between these living things and the non-living things around them. They wonder how certain plants and animals survive in particular places. They think about how one change, such as an increase in temperature or rainfall, might cause other changes. They examine ways that creatures depend on one another, and ways they compete. These scientists are called **ecologists**.

Some insects, like this hover fly, eat pollen and nectar from flowers. They often **pollinate** *the flowers they feed.*

When black-eyed Susans go to seed, they provide food for goldfinches and other seed-eaters.

The word **ecology** comes from the Greek word for house. You can think of ecology as the study of plants and animals at home, in their natural environment. This book will help you learn about the ecology of woods, ponds, and fields. It will help you explore the relationships and connections that exist within these special places.

7

The Woods

Woods are places where lots of trees grow. Shady and cool, they are special places to explore. Some woods are filled with evergreen **conifers**, like pines, firs, and hemlocks. Others have broad-leaved **deciduous** trees, like oaks and maples, that lose their leaves in autumn. Many woodlands have both kinds of trees. What are the woods like where you live?

Telling trees apart

Most woodlands contain many different kinds of plants. Ferns, mosses, and tiny wildflowers carpet the ground, and various shrubs and saplings stand over them. Then, of course, there are the trees. Each kind, or **species**, has characteristics that will help you tell it apart from others. Choose a tree to study, and look carefully at the shape of its leaves, and the color and texture of the bark. Then look to see if you can find other trees like it nearby.

Maple trees have broad leaves with several large parts, or lobes. Elms have oblong leaves with many small "teeth" along the edges.

Often, a few species of trees dominate a woodland; that is, they outnumber other species, and take up the most space. Ecologists describe woodlands according to their dominant trees. For example, you may live near an oak-pine forest, a spruce forest, a beech-maple forest, or a redwood forest.

Most oak trees can be put into one of two groups. Those in the white oak group have leaves with rounded lobes, and acorns that ripen within one year. Trees in the black oak group have leaves with pointed lobes, and acorns that take two years to mature.

You can make leaf or bark rubbings to help you remember the different trees you find. Sketches that show the basic shape of a tree, or details like flowers or buds, are also helpful. A field guide to the trees will help you name the trees you have learned to recognize.

A young green heron perches in oak tree.

ANIMALS IN

Lots of animals live in the woods. Yet it's possible to visit the woods and see very few. Why? Where are they?

Hide and seek

It's easy for people to overlook woodland animals because a lot of our everyday behavior is frightening to them. The sounds of people walking, talking, laughing, and whistling sends many animals running for cover. Also, we are most likely to visit the woods during the daytime. Yet some animals are nocturnal, or active at night, while others are crepuscular, or active at dawn and dusk. Some creatures are so small we tend to overlook them. Others go about their business underground, under tree bark, or in other places where we can't see them. If you want to find animals that live in the woods, here are some things you can try:

Salamanders hide under logs and litter.

Insects that tunnel inside leaves are often called "leaf miners."

If you find a dead branch on the ground, gently break it open. You may find a colony of termites living inside.

Some caterpillars live inside a folded leaf they have fastened together with silk. Look for leaf rollers next time you are in the woods.

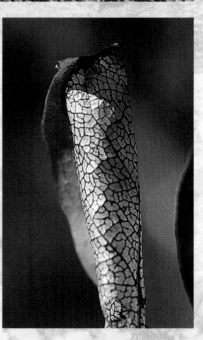

THE WOODS

stay quiet, get settled, get comfortable, and watch awhile. Birds, squirrels, and other animals that hide when they hear your crackling footsteps will often become active again as soon as sounds of danger have passed. If you remain motionless and quiet, they may come quite close.

Call to them. Once in a while, it helps to make noise! Birdwatchers have found that when they say "psh-psh-psh," songbirds hidden among trees often hop out to the ends of branches to check out the noise. For best results, try "pshing" when you have noticed birds nearby, and after you have stopped moving and talking.

Think small. Slugs, snails, spiders, and centipedes can all be found in the woods if you carefully inspect the ground, leaves, and tree bark around you.

Look for traces. Many animals leave signs that let you know where they have been. Learning to spot and read these signs can also help you learn what animals have been eating and doing. Some signs to look for are: tracks (footprints), scats (droppings), feathers, chewed or scratched twigs or bark, nibbled leaves, nests, and holes in trees or in the ground.

Lichens

Pale green lichens growing from the branches of a dead tree.

O n your next visit to the woods, look around for lichens. Tree trunks are one good place to look; lichens often form round, gray-green patches on tree bark. Some lichens hang like hair from tree branches, others grow on rotting stumps and logs. You can also check on the ground and on rocks. Lichens grow in many different places.

Some birds, like the blue-gray gnatcatcher, use lichens to build their nests.

Look for lichens on tree trunks (inset). You can also see fruticose lichens growing on a shingled roof.

But what are they?

It's easier to learn to recognize a lichen than to understand what one is, because a lichen is really two different kinds of organisms living together. One is a **fungus** (grouped with mushrooms, puffballs, and

molds). The other is a green or blue-green **alga**. (Seaweeds are familiar, large-sized algae. There are many

GREEN POND ALGAE

microscopic varieties as well.) If you cut a thin sliver from a lichen and look at it under a microscope, you can actually see the tiny algal cells surrounded by fungus.

The algae and fungi that combine to form lichens have evolved together for millions of years. The algae provide the fungi with the **carbohydrates**, or sugars, they need in order to grow. Like trees and other green plants, algae can make this food. The blue-green algae within some lichens fix, or collect, nitrogen from the air. The fixed nitrogen then nourishes the fungi. It's not entirely clear whether these algae benefit from their association with fungi; perhaps living inside a fungus keeps them from drying out. Scientists use the word **commensalism** to describe partnerships like this, where one organism benefits and neither is hurt.

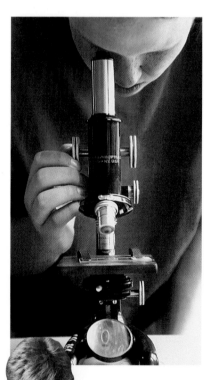

A hand lens or a dissecting microscope will give you a close-up view of a lichen.

Classifying lichens

There are at least 17,000 species of lichens in the world. They can be sorted into three basic groups:

CRUSTOSE

Crustose lichens grow in a flat, crusty layer.

FOLIOSE

Foliose lichens have a leafy or leathery look.

FRUTICOSE

Fruticose lichens often look moss-like, or like little bushes.

Many scientists think of fungi as plants, and include them in the plant **kingdom**. Other scientists place fungi in a kingdom of their own, separating them from green plants because they cannot **photosynthesize**, or make their own food. Similarly, green and blue-green algae are sometimes thought of as plants, but are often included in other kingdoms. What's to be done with a lichen, an organism that's part fungus and part alga?

Air quality indicators

Lichens can live for many years under the right conditions. Some researchers think certain patches of lichen in the Arctic may be thousands of years old! However, lichens are slow-growing, and most are sensitive to chemicals in the air. In places where the air contains high levels of sulphur dioxide and other pollutants, most lichens cannot grow. As you move away from a heavily polluted area, you'll begin to find crustose species. Continue on, and foliose lichens occur as well. Fruticose lichens are the most sensitive to pollution. Their presence indicates very clean air.

FRUTICOSE LICHEN

Making Leaf Prints

 ou can use leaf prints to record the shape and pattern of veins you notice in different kinds of leaves, or to create beautiful designs on paper, T-shirts, or other surfaces. If you are printing on fabric, make sure to use acrylic paint or a printing ink that will not wash out when the fabric is laundered. Experiment with different leaves, inks, and printing surfaces to see what effects you like best.

Materials:

- newspaper
- acrylic paint or water-base printing ink*
- tray, or pane of glass with taped edges
- brayer (the ink roller)*
- leaves
- paper or cloth

*ACRYLIC PAINT, INK, AND BRAYERS ARE AVAILABLE AT ART SUPPLY STORES. IF YOU ARE PRINTING ON FABRIC, MAKE SURE TO USE ACRYLIC PAINT OR A PRINTING INK THAT WILL NOT WASH OUT WHEN THE FABRIC IS WASHED.

Directions:

1. Cover your work space with a layer of old newspaper.

2. Squeeze a small amount of ink onto the tray or glass.

3. Roll the brayer in the ink to coat it.

4. Place a leaf on a sheet of newspaper. Use the brayer to coat the leaf with ink. If you coat the underside of the leaf, the veins will print more clearly.

5. Press down on the leaf with your fingers. Try to press each part of it. Put the leaf, ink side down, on a piece of paper or fabric.

6. Remove the leaf by slowly pulling the stem and edges straight up off the paper or cloth.

SNAGS

Long after a tree has died, it continues to provide food and shelter for woodland animals. Inspect these dead trees, called snags, carefully. The nests, holes, and tunnels you find will help you figure out what creatures are using it. Dead and dying trees support lichens, fungi, and other green plants, as well as animals.

16

Microscopic algae often turn bark and dead wood green.

The row of small holes in this birch bark was probably made by a yellow-bellied sapsucker, back when the tree was still alive. The holes sapsuckers make sometimes allow a disease organisms to infect a tree.

A large hole may turn out to be the entrance to a woodpecker's nest. Many woodpeckers also make smaller, shallower holes as they dig for carpenter ants, wood-boring beetle larvae, and other insects that infest trees.

No bird made this hole. It formed naturally when a branch fell off the tree.

This is a young downy woodpecker. As an adult, it may chisel a nest cavity in a dead or dying tree.

The common flicker nests in dead snags, stumps, and live trees, but typically looks for food on the ground.

Cavity nesters

The common flicker, *Colaptes auratus*, is a cavity nester. Like other woodpeckers, it uses its strong beak to hollow out a chamber within a tree. Though the entrance to a flicker's nest is a hole just a few inches wide, the chamber it leads to may be two or three feet deep. It takes a pair of flickers a week or two to excavate a new cavity. Sometimes they'll fix up an old one rather than starting from scratch. Flickers nest in open woodlands. They make use of live trees, dead snags, and stumps. Unlike most other woodpeckers, flickers often dig in the ground for insects to eat.

This hole was made by a woodpecker, though another bird may now be nesting in the cavity it leads to.

Woodpeckers are not the only cavity nesters: kestrels, nuthatches, titmice, chickadees, bluebirds, starlings, and other birds also lay eggs in hollowed-out trees or stumps. Most cannot tunnel into wood themselves, but move into natural hollows, or those made by wood-peckers. Flickers and other cavity-makers often end up providing nest sites for a variety of species. If you find a woodpecker hole, observe it frequently. You may be able to spot its current inhabitant on the way in or out.

Some cavity-makers take weather into account when deciding where, and how, to build. You may find more woodpeck-er holes in the protected sides of trees than facing into prevailing winds. The holes may be directed downward as well, to help keep out rain.

17

Keep an eye on any cavities you find, to see if birds are nesting inside. A pair of starlings are raising a family in this natural tree cavity.

Underfoot

Many people rake up fallen leaves in the autumn, **composting** them, or bagging them up to be taken to a landfill. In the woods, fallen leaves pile up on the ground. Together with broken branches, seeds, and dead animals, they form a spongy layer that ecologists call **litter**. Leaf litter is an important part of the woods. It holds soil in place, preventing heavy rains and high winds from **eroding** it, or carrying it away. Litter keeps the soil beneath it moist by shielding it from drying sun and wind, and by gradually releasing soaked-up rain water.

Sifting slowly and carefully through the layers of leaf litter will help you find animals like this earthworm.

Over time, small animals, fungi, and microorganisms that live in the litter cause it to rot, or decay. Organisms responsible for decay are called **decomposers**. Animals break large leaves into smaller pieces as they move about. They also eat dead leaves, branches, and animals, digest them, and eventually excrete much of what they've eaten. Many fungi and microorganisms secrete special digestive chemicals onto the litter, and absorb the nutritious liquid that results from digested leaves and animal waste. These activities create a layer of soil called **humus**, rich with the nutrients that help trees grow.

LEAF LITTER SURFACE

SECOND LAYER—BROKEN LEAVES

SOIL/HUMUS BENEATH LITTER

Life in the litter

You can find out what lives in litter by gently sifting through some of it with your fingers. Look under pieces of bark, or break open fallen twigs and branches. Look for slugs, insects, and other small animals, and for the fine, root-like **hyphae** of fungi. Some of the organisms you

find will be decomposers. You will also find predators that come to feed on the litter-eaters. You may see chewed leaves, tiny spider webs, and other signs of animal activity, even when you do not see the animals themselves. Look for changes in the size and color of litter or soil particles as you dig deeper and deeper, and keep track of the animals you find at different levels.

Raising earthworms

Earthworms live in many places, including woodlands. They aren't common in acidic soil, so you're more apt to find them where there are broad-leaved trees like oaks and maples, rather than acid-loving pines and cedars. Fallen leaves are an important part of an earthworm's diet. Like many other soil animals, they help break down leaf litter and recycle the nutrients it contains.

Housing: You can raise earthworms in a dish pan, picnic cooler, or gallon glass jar. Fill your container with loose, moist soil. Use soil that is high in organic matter, rather than sand or clay. If you gather soil from the same spot you collect worms, you know it will suit them. Keep the container away from direct sunlight, and mist the soil with

water if it starts to dry out. Make a cardboard cover with holes for ventilation. A one gallon jar will house ten or twelve worms. Larger containers can hold many more.

Food: Earthworms eat fresh and decaying plants they find around their burrows, and organic matter in the soil. Feed your worms every other week by sprinkling moist cornmeal or bread crumbs on top of the soil. You can also add a few leaves to the container. Remove uneaten food before it rots.

Habits: If you want to observe mating or feeding, you'll probably need to make observations at night. During the day, you can unearth a few worms and place them on damp paper toweling in order to get a closer look at them.

What Owls Eat

©PHOTO CORNELL LABORATORY OF ORNITHOLOGY

If you've ever been near the woods at night, you may have heard an owl call. Each species has a distinctive call, so it is possible to find out what kinds of owls live near you just by listening. All owls are predators, but since different species have different diets, more than one kind of owl may live in a particular woodland without competing for the same food.

©PHOTO CORNELL LABORATORY OF ORNITHOLOGY

Great horned owls prey on rabbits and other small animals.

You may find that the easiest way to get a good, close look at an owl is to visit a museum.

What owls eat

Great horned owls hunt for mice, rabbits, and other small mammals in the woods at night. Though mammals are their principal food, they also eat beetles, frogs, lizards, and birds. Barred owls eat small mammals, too, though in southern swampy woodlands crayfish, frogs, and fish are the mainstays of their diet. The smaller screech owl usually feeds on insects.

How did people figure out what these nocturnal hunters eat? Some people have actually observed owls at night, and seen them catch and eat prey. People also learn about animal diets by examining droppings and **pellets**. Owls tend to swallow their prey whole, or to tear off and gulp down large pieces. When an owl eats a mouse, it swallows it—fur, bones, and all. The fur and bones aren't nutritious or digestible, however, and they are regurgitated, or thrown up, a few hours later, pressed together in a pellet.

You might find an owl pellet when you are walking in the woods. Sometimes a few will be piled up under an owl's favorite perch. You can also buy pellets to study. Wildlife centers that rehabilitate injured owls often collect them from captive birds.

RODENT SKULL

Dissecting an owl pellet

1. If your pellet is dry, soak it in water for a few minutes to soften the fur and feathers.

2. Use your fingers, toothpicks, or a probe and forceps to gently tease apart the pellet.

3. Separate bones, teeth, and other hard material from soft fur and feathers and clean them with a damp sponge.

4. You can use a book about bones, or a field guide to mammals, to help you identify some of the bones you find.

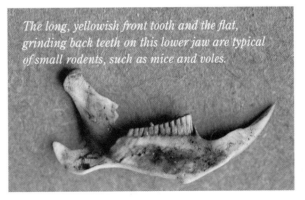

The long, yellowish front tooth and the flat, grinding back teeth on this lower jaw are typical of small rodents, such as mice and voles.

5. Mount the bones on poster board or construction paper, or try to reconstruct a skeleton from bones that seem like they might have come from the same animal.

21

Box Turtles

The eastern box turtle, *Terrapene carolina,* lives in woodlands, pastures, fields, and dunes. Occasionally you may see one in the water, but they are basically **terrestrial** animals. For this reason, some people call them tortoises instead of turtles.

Homebodies and wanderers

Young box turtles often establish a territory, or **home range**, and remain there for decades. This home range may measure just a few hundred yards in diameter. If you find a box turtle, watch it for a while, then leave it exactly where you found it. If you remove it from its home range and release it elsewhere, it may try to get back. This could be an impossible job for a small, slow-moving animal, unable to dodge road traffic.

Scientists have discovered that not all box turtles stay within a fixed home range. Some seem to be wanderers, passing through the home ranges of others as they travel.

Bones on the inside, bones on the outside

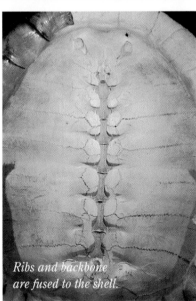

Ribs and backbone are fused to the shell.

A turtle's shell is made of bone, covered with a layer of thick skin or horn-like material. The ribs and backbone are fused to the bones of the shell. A real turtle cannot crawl out of its shell, as cartoon turtles do, because its shell and the rest of its skeleton are connected. The colors and markings on a turtle's shell can help you identify it.

This is the posterior lobe of a male plastron.

Telling males and females apart

You can usually tell the sex of a box turtle by looking at its eyes. Females have brown eyes, while males typically have reddish ones. You can also tell males and females apart by looking at the **plastron**, or bottom shell. The plastron has a line across it separating the **anterior** (front) lobe from the larger **posterior** (rear) lobe. Look carefully at the posterior lobe. If it is flat or bulges out slightly, the turtle is a female. If it is slightly concave, or dented in, the turtle is a male. The top shell, or **carapace**, of the female is usually more rounded, while the male has a flatter carapace with a more sharply defined notch at the neck.

Closing the box

Box turtles have remarkable shells. The line between the two lobes of the plastron is actually a hinge, and the plastron is attached to the carapace with ligaments rather than immovable bone. *Terrapene carolina* can pull in its head and legs, then press each lobe of the plastron against the carapace so tightly that no soft tissue is exposed. Most turtles cannot "close" their shells like this.

The box turtle's special shell is an **adaptation** that protects it from larger animals that might otherwise eat it. Adaptations are physical characteristics or behaviors that help living things survive.

A long life

A female box turtle lays her eggs in spring or early summer. She puts them in a hole dug in soft ground, covers them, and leaves. When the baby turtles hatch, they are completely independent. They crawl off in search of food and a place to live. Box turtles eat mushrooms, berries, leaves, seeds, and many kinds of low-growing plants. They also eat insects, snails, and other small animals. Predators, like skunks and crows, will dig up box turtle eggs and prey on hatchlings, but large box turtles are seldom bothered by

other wild animals. With luck, they may live half a century or more.

You can estimate the age of a box turtle by counting the annual growth rings on one of its **scutes**, the plates that form the outer layer of the shell. Young turtles are easier to age than older ones. An older turtle's growth rings may be worn and indistinct, or there may be so many they are difficult to count. A magnifying glass will help you.

Homes on the range

Box turtles live in parts of the eastern and midwestern United States and Canada. There is also a western species of box turtle. Once common, these animal are now protected in some states. Though adult box turtles have few natural enemies, human activity has reduced their numbers. Turtles fare badly when roads and housing developments criss-cross their habitat, and when people collect them, or move them from their home ranges.

Using a Berlese Funnel

A Berlese funnel (also called a Tullgren funnel) can help you find out what animals live in leaf litter and soil. It will help you collect very tiny animals that you might otherwise overlook. You can make your own Berlese funnel from equipment you buy or find around the house, or you can order a funnel from one of the companies listed on page 62.

Materials

- a large plastic or metal funnel
- glass vial, just big enough to fit over the narrow end of the funnel (optional)
- piece of coarse wire screen (a 1 centimeter or 1/4 inch mesh will do)
- wire cutters or tin snips
- jar, bucket, or three-legged stand to hold funnel
- some leaf litter or soil, freshly collected
- a gooseneck lamp, or an adjustable desk lamp
- jar lid or petri dish

Directions

1. Cut a circular piece from the wire screen with the wire cutters or tin snips. Make the circle three or more inches in diameter.
2. If you are using a purchased funnel that comes with a glass collecting vial, slip the vial onto the small end of the funnel.

3. Place the circular screen inside the funnel.

4. Set the funnel on the three-legged stand, or place it in a jar or bucket that will hold the funnel upright.

5. Fill the funnel several inches deep with leaf litter. Make sure to use fresh litter that you've collected that day.

6. Turn on the lamp, and position it so that the bulb shines down onto the leaf litter. Make sure the bulb is close enough to warm the litter, but not positioned in a way that might melt a plastic funnel!

7. After half an hour or so, lift the funnel and look into the collecting vial, bucket, or jar. If no animals are present, set the funnel back under the light and wait a while longer. You may want to check your funnel frequently at first to see how long it takes for animals to begin dropping into the jar. You can leave your funnel under the light for as long as you want, provided you are nearby.

8. Study the creatures you have collected. You might want to put some in a jar lid or plastic petri dish so that you can observe them with a hand lens or microscope. You will probably find animals that are new to you, as well as some familiar ones.

9. When you are through, return the animals you collected to the litter or soil they crawled out of. Put the litter or soil back where you found it.

Real Pseudo

You may find a pseudoscorpion among the animals you collect with your Berlese funnel. Although pseudoscorpions are common in leaf litter, they are so small that people usually don't notice them. Most pseudoscorpions are less than two-tenths of an inch long. Though they do have fierce-looking pincers, they are too small to pinch or bite a person. They prey on tiny insects.

Note: You can use a mothball instead of a light bulb to drive the animals out of the litter. Simply tape a mothball to a piece of wood or cardboard large enough to cover the open top of your funnel. Place the board on the funnel, with the mothball "inside," over the litter. Use the funnel outdoors, on the porch, or in another well-ventilated area, since it isn't healthy to inhale mothball fumes.

Fields

 ields are open stretches of land where crops, grasses, or wildflowers grow.

The plants that grow in a field get lots of sun. Some fields occur naturally. Others are created when people clear trees from land in order to build or plant crops.

Flowering grass

What are flowers?

We appreciate flowers for their beauty, but they are not merely decorative. Flowers contain special organs that can produce seeds, the means by which many plants reproduce. Not all plants have flowers, but lots of familiar ones do. Some are large and showy. Others, like the flowers on certain trees and grasses, are often overlooked.

Black-eyed Susans (above) are common in fields and along roadsides in the midwestern and eastern United States. The dark brown center of each "flower" is actually a cluster of many tiny flowers.

Changes

A field may have dozens of different wildflowers in bloom at once. You may notice that a few seem to dominate the landscape, while others are few in number, or hidden underneath larger, bolder, blossoms. Which flowers are common in the fields near your home?

Each kind of flower blooms at a particular time. Dandelions bloom in spring and early summer, while goldenrod flowers from late summer to fall. As you get familiar with a field, you will start to notice that when one type of flower wilts, another comes into bloom. Keep track of the patterns you notice. You may see connections between the lives of the birds and insects you observe in a field, and the flowers you have been watching. The American goldfinch, for example, has an unusually late nesting season, from July through September. Sunflowers, thistles, and many other wildflowers have developed seeds by late summer, providing a good supply of food for the adult goldfinches and their growing young.

PLANTS TO

Before you set out to learn about plant ecology, find out if there are any plants in your area you should handle with care, or look at from a distance!

Stinging Nettles, above, and Poison Ivy, right.

Poison ivy, poison oak

Poison Ivy growing on a tree

Poison ivy, **Rhus radicans**, is common in many parts of North America. You can find it in woods, fields, parks, yards, and along roads and beaches. Poison oak, **Rhus diversiloba**, looks similar to poison ivy. It is a closely related species that is found in the western United States.

Many people are allergic to the oil that coats poison oak and ivy. They break out in an itchy rash if they touch a plant directly, or handle an object that has brushed against one. Learn to recognize poison oak and ivy so your outdoor explorations don't leave you scratching! It's wise to avoid touching these plants even if you are not allergic to them, because sometimes allergies develop through repeated exposure to irritating substances.

Recognizing poison ivy

Poison ivy is a plant with compound leaves. It has a group of leaflets attached to one petiole, or stem. Poison ivy leaflets come in groups of three. The leaflets are often asymmetrical; one side may have several bumps, or "teeth," along the edge, while the other side is fairly smooth. The leaves may be a dark, rich green, but sometimes they have a reddish cast. Poison ivy can form a low-growing ground cover, or creep high up tree trunks. A few plants may be scattered and widely spaced, or many can grow together.

In late summer you may notice berries developing among the foliage. In autumn, after the leaves have turned color and fallen, you can still find the woody stems full of creamy white berries. Though they are pretty to look at, the stems and berries can cause a rash just as easily as the leaves can. It's best to avoid poison ivy at all times of year!

WATCH OUT FOR

Poison Oak

© PHOTO HARPER HORTICULTURAL SLIDE LIBRARY

Precautions

Learning to recognize and avoid irritating plants will keep you from getting some uncomfortable rashes. You can also wear shoes, long pants, and a long-sleeved shirt when exploring places that are heavily infested with poison oak or ivy. If you accidentally brush against some, or handle a ball or insect net that touched it, wash thoroughly with soap and water when you get home. Often, you can remove the oil from your skin before it causes any trouble. Also, be sure to throw your clothes in the washing machine right away.

Stinging nettles

The stinging nettle, *Urtica dioica*, is common in fields, vacant lots, and along roadsides in many areas. Stinging nettles are covered with tiny hairs filled with formic acid. If you accidentally brush against a nettle, the acid will sting your skin.

It is well worth learning to move carefully around nettles, so that you can study the animals that depend on them. The red admiral butterfly, *Vanessa atalanta*, often lays her eggs on nettle plants. When the eggs hatch, the growing caterpillars eat the nettle leaves. When a caterpillar is fully grown, it pulls the sides of a leaf together and fastens them with silk. The folded leaf, covered with its acid-filled hairs, makes a safe place for the larvae to pupate. You may notice other kinds of insects, and spiders, living on nettle plants. Ecologists call a group of organisms that live together in the same place a community.

RED ADMIRAL LARVA ON NETTLES

RED ADMIRAL PUPA ON NETTLES

RED ADMIRAL ADULT ON NETTLES

Collecting and

Botanists, the scientists who study plants, sometimes collect leaves and flowers to press. The pressed specimens are a useful record of the different species that grow in a particular area.

Field notes

Take note of details that will help you remember and identify the plants you collect. How big was the plant? Where was it growing? What color were the flowers and leaves? Pressed specimens look faded and flat compared to freshly collected ones, so good notes and sketches are important!

Making a herbarium

Pressing dries and preserves plant specimens. Mounted, identified, and labeled, a collection of pressed specimens makes up a **herbarium**. Herbariums are useful to researchers and students who want to learn more about different kinds of plants. You can make your own herbarium. First, make yourself a plant press.

Collecting plants

You can use a scissors or pocket knife to cut your own specimens. If you are collecting grasses or wildflowers, cut a long enough piece of stem to get both blossoms and leaves. Some flowers can be collected throughout the day, but others must be cut early because they wilt or close up in the afternoon.

Find out if any plants in your area are rare and should not be collected. Check with a local nature center, or consult a list of protected species to find out. Also make sure you recognize poison ivy and other irritating plants that are best left alone!

Pressing Plants

You'll need:

- Newspaper.
- Five or ten pieces of corrugated cardboard, 8"x10" or larger.*
- White construction paper or blotter paper.
- Two pieces of Masonite, very stiff cardboard, or end boards made of wooden slats. These should be the same size as the corrugated cardboard, or slightly larger.
- Two straps with buckles, or with Velcro sewn on as a fastener.
- * A plant press can be any size you find useful. Try making a large one to keep at home, and a pocket size one to carry with you.

Place the end boards on the top and bottom of your layers of cardboard and paper.

Directions:

1. Put a few layers of newspaper on top of a piece of corrugated cardboard. Add two sheets of white paper and another layer of newspaper.
2. Repeat these steps, beginning with a new piece of cardboard, until you have only one piece of cardboard left.
3. Top off your stack with a final layer of cardboard, then sandwich the entire stack between the two pieces of Masonite, stiff cardboard, or end boards.
4. Use the straps to fasten the whole package together. Your plant press is ready to use!

Pressing your specimens

Open your plant press, and arrange your specimens between the pieces of white construction paper or blotting paper. Take care to keep plants from overlapping one another, or they will stick together and tear when you try to separate them. When all your specimens are positioned, fasten the straps of the press tightly. In a week or two you may open the press and remove the dry specimens.

A stack of books is a good substitute for straps.

Mounting pressed plants

Dried specimens can be glued or taped to heavy paper, or mounted under a layer of clear, adhesive-backed plastic. Botanists usually record the scientific name of each specimen in a herbarium, and group each plant with closely related species. Record the name of each plant you are able to identify on the paper that you mounted it on. Keep your collection in a notebook or folder.

MOUNTING

LABELING

31

Ticks

Ticks are small animals that spend much of their time sitting around on leaves or weeds. They don't fly, or even crawl around very much. Ticks can go a long, long time without food. Some can do without a meal for an entire year!

Ticks are small and dark, and often hard to see. Can you find the tick near the center of this photo?

How do ticks eat?

Ticks are **parasites**. When they do eat, they suck blood from other animals. Some ticks parasitize birds and reptiles, while others parasitize mammals. A tick doesn't actively search for a host, it just waits. An appropriate animal that brushes against the vegetation where a tick is resting may soon become host to a hungry tick. Once on board, the

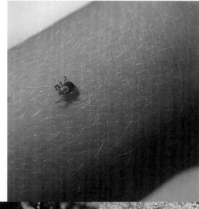

tick sticks specialized mouthparts through the host's skin and begins to suck its blood. Ticks have expandable bodies. As they feed, their bodies swell. An engorged tick may be several times its pre-meal size. When it has drunk its fill, the tick withdraws its mouthparts and drops onto a plant or the ground. It molts, then waits around for a new host to pass by.

Mating

Male
5X life size

Female
5X life size

You can tell male and female ticks of many species apart because the males' bodies are covered with a shiny, hard plate. Females have a much smaller plate near the head, while the rear part of their bodies is wrinkled, or leathery-looking. Males and females find each other when they are feeding on the same host. They mate while still on the host, then drop off. Females lay their eggs on the ground, then crawl onto a plant to molt and wait for a new host to pass by.

When tick eggs hatch, the tiny larvae that emerge from them have only three pairs of jointed legs, rather than four. Eventually, they will develop another pair. Some people call these young ticks "seed ticks."

Tick problems

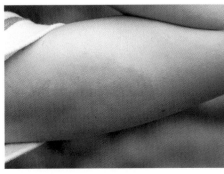

All ticks are parasites, and some species parasitize us! This is a problem if the ticks that bite us carry certain germs—infected ticks can spread disease. Rocky Mountain spotted fever and Lyme disease are both carried to people by ticks.

You can reduce your chances of being bitten by a tick if you wear long pants when hiking or playing in areas where ticks live. Tuck your pants into your socks at the ankle to prevent ticks from crawling up a loose pant leg. Long sleeves and turned-up collars also help. If you wear light-colored clothing instead of dark, it's easier to see ticks that land on you. Check yourself for ticks, or have a friend check, when you leave a tick-infested area. Brush off any ticks you find.

Lyme disease

Some ticks are very tiny. *Ixodes dammini*, the deer tick that spreads Lyme disease, is only about the size of a poppy seed! You may not spot such a small tick even if one lands on you, and you probably won't feel it bite, either. But if you notice a strange-looking rash on your skin, call a doctor. The rash might indicate that you have been bitten by a tick carrying the germs that cause Lyme disease. If left alone, the rash will go away, but fever, joint pains, and other symptoms may occur. Early treatment can keep serious complications from developing.

Ticks are easiest to spot on light-colored clothing.

This rash could mean Lyme disease. See a doctor!

SUMMER SINGERS

In late summer and early fall, fields are filled with the rhythmic chirping and trilling of thousands of insects. Sit quietly and listen. How many different sounds can you hear? Listen at different times during the day and night. Insects that are quiet at one time may be noisy at another.

Grasshopper Nymph

Who's making all that noise?

Some of the most familiar field sounds are the mating calls made by grasshoppers and crickets. Usually, it's the males who sing, but in some species males and females call to each other. Grasshoppers make sounds by rubbing their hind legs against their wings, while crickets rub a ridge on one wing across a scraper on the other. There are many species of grasshoppers and crickets, and each has a different call. Even when you can't spot the singer, you may recognize its song.

Finding grasshoppers and field crickets

You may notice grasshoppers chewing on plant stems, or they may surprise you as they jump or fly out of your way. Look for crickets on the ground, under litter or stones, and in piles of grass clippings, hay, or weeds.

Female Cricket

In warm climates you can find these insects throughout the year. In cooler climates, where autumn frosts kill the adults, they overwinter as eggs in the ground. In the spring, the young, called nymphs, emerge from the eggs. By mid-summer many nymphs have matured, and adults are again plentiful. If you can, catch a few nymphs or adults. They are easy to raise, and interesting to watch.

If you're quick, you may be able to catch a grasshopper with your bare hands.

Raising grasshoppers and field crickets

Food: Crickets can eat an enormous variety of things: plants, other insects, even cloth and leather! Dry dog food pellets are another food possibility for captive crickets. You can vary their diet with small slices of fruit and vegetables. Give grasshoppers fresh leaves from grasses and other field plants, or green vegetables. Make sure you remove old food before it starts to rot.

Numbers: Crickets and grasshoppers need plenty of space. Too many in one container may cause them to be aggressive and injure one another. Male crickets often claim a particular territory, make sounds to warn others away, and chase or kick intruders. If your container is small (a one-gallon fish tank, for example) keep only one male and a female or two. Larger containers, well supplied with hiding places and things to crawl on, can hold more.

Behavior to look for

What do crickets and grasshoppers do? Watch carefully to see. You may notice

- eating
- drinking
- grooming
- chirping
- responses to chirping
- mating
- egg laying

Compare the observations you make indoors to those you make in the field. It is much easier to observe a grasshopper or cricket over time when you bring it indoors, but captive animals do not always behave just as they would in the wild.

Housing: Keep grasshoppers and crickets in glass or clear plastic containers. Add a tight-fitting top made from wire screening or cheesecloth. Layer an inch or two of sand, soil, or peat moss on the bottom of the container so that females will have a place to lay their eggs. Sterilize the soil by baking it at 200 degrees for two hours, so bacteria and fungi will be slower to grow. Mist the soil with water, and check it periodically. Some moisture will encourage females to lay eggs, and it may help the eggs develop, but they won't hatch if the soil is really wet. Add a few stones, cardboard tubes, or other "hiding places."

Water: A clean piece of sponge plugged into a small bottle of water will provide a continuing supply of water. A jar lid containing a wet piece of sponge, or a few drops of water sprinkled on rocks or food will work as well.

Different Animals...

Different kinds of animals require different living conditions. Some thrive in sunshine, while others need protection from excessive light and heat. Some require lots of moisture, others suffer if they get too wet. Light, temperature, and other factors can vary from place to place, even within one small area. How many different living places can you find in a field?

The color of this bug makes it hard to spot as it crawls on a grass plant.

Thornhoppers suck the juice from a flower stem.

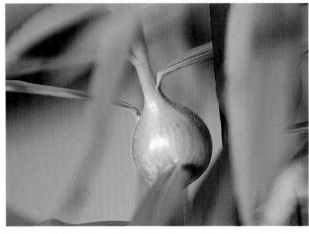

This swollen goldenrod stem harbors a tiny insect larva, and protects it from the elements. Swellings like this one are called galls.

Check the undersides of leaves as well as their tops. You may find animals on one side that you do not find on the other.

Different Living Conditions

The underside of this milkweed leaf is covered with tiny, sap-sucking aphids.

This hole is the entrance to a woodchuck's burrow. The woodchuck looks for food in the field early in the morning and late in the afternoon, but spends the rest of the day underground.

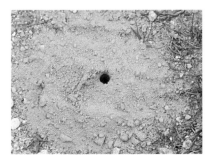

Ants have colonized the sandy soil of this field.

Changing the environment

Sometimes, people deliberately or unknowingly change a particular habitat in ways that make it attractive to some organisms, but less suitable for others. For example, a piece of heavy plastic can create a haven for slugs, land snails, and other moisture-loving invertebrates. It can also provide a wasp with mud to build an egg case. Experiment to see what happens when you change a small patch of ground by covering it with a wooden board or shingle. What animals do you find there before you position the shingle? What is underneath after a day or two? After a week or two?

Change the living conditions on a patch of ground by covering it with a board.

BIRDWATCHING

Birdwatching is a favorite hobby for many people, as well as a way for ornithologists (scientists who study birds) to collect information. Most birds nest and look for food in particular places. Explore different habitats to see what kind of birds live there.

When to go, what to take

Try looking and listening for birds at different times of the day. Some birds start singing before dawn, others call at sunset. Birds don't stick to "business hours," so you may have to change your schedule to find some of the birds that live near you.

© PHOTO CORNELL LABORATORY OF ORNITHOLOGY

You do not need any special equipment to start birdwatching. Some birds are large and easy to see, and many will come quite close to you if you are still and quiet. If you get serious about birdwatching, you will probably want to buy binoculars. There are many kinds, so talk to experienced birdwatchers to find out what type they find most useful. Binoculars have numbers printed on them that tell you about their capabilities. Most birdwatchers prefer a pair that can magnify an image 7-8.5 times, with the largest lenses measuring 35-50 mm. Check the field of vision, too. You'll want a pair with a reasonably wide angle (more than 7 degrees, or 350 feet/1000 yards). Binoculars with a single focusing knob are easiest to use.

An ordinary pair of binoculars can take you up close to a robin feeding its young (above), or allow you to follow a flock on the wing (right).

What to look for

This gray catbird has an insect in its beak. It probably has a nest full of hungry young nearby.

When a bird, like this yellowthroat, preens, it uses its beak to smooth and oil its feathers.

A bird's song may help it attract a mate or establish a territory. This singer is a Carolina wren.

Watch the way birds act. Behaviors like flying, eating, preening, and singing help birds survive and reproduce. Some behaviors send a message to other birds. Sometimes you can figure out the meaning of a behavior by watching the way other birds respond to it. Take note of where you see particular kinds of birds. You may see flickers feeding on the ground in a yard or park, but locate their nests in dead trees in the woods. Many birds make use of more than one kind of area, or habitat. You can also look for the unique aspects of a bird's appearance that distinguish it from other kinds of birds. A field guide to birds will point out these field marks, and help you identify birds.

Flickers often feed on the ground. They eat ants and other insects. Look for their nests in dead trees.

Adult mute swans, Cygnus olor, stay with their young for several months after they hatch and defend them from potential predators. These behaviors help insure the survival of the cygnets.

A black head and neck and white "chin strap" are field marks of the Canada goose, Branta canadensis.

Goldfinches

 oldfinches are common in many parts of North America. Watch for them in fields, gardens, along roadsides, and at bird feeders. Goldfinches are seed eaters; their short, sturdy beaks are good at picking and hulling. Weeds, wildflowers, and trees provide them with food.

Field birds

Look for the American goldfinch, *Carduelis tristus*, when you visit a field. Males are easiest to recognize, for in spring and summer their bright yellow feathers make them stand out. Female goldfinches have black wings with a white bar or stripe, like males do, but their backs and heads are a muted olive green. When summer is over, goldfinches **molt**, or replace old, worn feathers with new ones. Both males and females turn a dull grayish color, though they keep the characteristic white stripe on their dark wings.

In spring and summer, you can tell males from females by their color.

This male goldfinch blends in almost perfectly with the wildflowers whose seeds he feeds on.

Raising a family

Altricial young are completely dependent on their parents. These are baby bluebirds.

The goldfinch nesting season begins in July and extends into September. Nests are built in trees or bushes, and lined with soft plant fibers such as milkweed, cattail, or thistle down. A female goldfinch lays four to six tiny eggs in her nest, and **incubates**, or sits on them, for about two weeks. Her mate brings food to her while she keeps the eggs warm.

Goldfinches and other songbirds have **altricial** young, that is, poorly developed hatchlings that are completely dependent on their parents. Newly hatched goldfinches have no feathers. They cannot fly, see, or find their own food. Their parents collect seeds and regurgitate them to feed the growing babies. Even after the young have **fledged**, or learned to fly, the parents will continue to feed them for a time.

Flight patterns

You can recognize a goldfinch by the color of its feathers, and you can also learn to recognize it by the way it flies. Different kinds of birds have different **flight patterns**, or ways of moving through the air. Some beat their wings a few times in a row then close them a moment, others flap slowly and steadily, and still others glide. Goldfinches have an undulating, or wavy, flight.

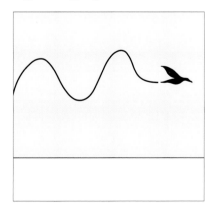

What's Your Niche?

In a pond, field, or in the woods, many kinds of plants and animals live near each other. These neighboring species have different ways of getting food and water, staying safe, and relating to other living things. Ecologists call a particular species' role within a community its **niche**.

It's a living

Some people think of an animal's niche as its job, or way of making a living. Words like "predator" or "prey" only partly define niches. To begin to understand a species' role in its community, you need to know exactly where, and how, it lives. What does it eat, and what impact does it have on its food source? In what ways does it change the place where it lives? Who are its enemies, and what defenses does it have against them? When is it active? When is it absent?

Of course, it's not possible to know everything about an animal! But thinking about a few aspects of its niche will help you see important relationships and connections in the world around you.

Each kind of pond animal occupies a different niche.

MELOSPIZA MELODIA

CARDUELIS TRISTUS

Neighbors

Some animals within a community seem quite similar to one another. For example, the goldfinch, *Carduelis tristus*, and the song sparrow, *Melospiza melodia*, both frequent brushy fields, farms, and gardens. Do these species share the same niche? Ecologists think not. Though there are areas where their niches overlap, there are also important differences in the way these two birds relate to their community.

MELOSPIZA MELODIA	CARDUELIS TRISTUS
• Sometimes build in a low bush or tree; often nest right on the ground.	• Nest in bushes and trees.
• Line nest with tiny roots, fine grass, and hair.	• Line nest with thistle or cattail down.
• Feed their young insects.	• Feed their young flower seeds.
• Adults eat seeds and insects.	• Adults are seed eaters.
• Wastes fertilize nearby plants, and sometimes transport seeds.	• Wastes fertilize nearby plants, and sometimes transport seeds.

One species—two niches

Damselfly nymph

Dragonfly nymph

An animal may fill a different niche as an adult than it did when it was young. Adult dragonflies prey on insects they catch as they fly through the air. Dragonfly and damselfly nymphs are predators, too, but they live and hunt under water.

Adult damselflies and dragonflies breathe air, and catch insects as they fly.

PONDS

Ponds are wet places with mucky bottoms. Some are full of water all year round; others dry up in the summer. Ponds are usually shallow enough for sunlight to reach all the way to the bottom. Ponds form in different ways. Some were formed as glaciers retreated during the last ice age, some are carved by streams and rivers, and some are made by people or other animals. Many fascinating plants and animals live in, on, and around ponds. Some simple equipment will help you to find and study them.

Things to bring

- Old sneakers or rubber boots will protect your feet from sharp stones and broken glass.
- An aquatic net or kitchen strainer is useful for scooping samples from the pond bottom.
- A plastic hand lens will give you a close-up view of the smaller plants or animals you find.
- Binoculars are great for watching birds and turtles.
- A shallow pan or plastic bucket makes a good temporary aquarium for any small aquatic animals that you want to observe awhile before releasing.
- White enamel refrigerator pans, or light-colored plastic dishpans will make your catch easy to see.

Remember to plan your pond trips with an adult so you will know where you can explore safely, and bring along a friend.
Collect pond animals from the shore or by wading in shallow water.

Changes

Pond water may turn green with algae in the summer, and freeze solid in winter. Animals that are common during one season may be difficult to find in another. Visit a pond at different times of the year to learn about these changes.

Pond Bank Predators

Many birds hunt for food in and around ponds. Some eat aquatic plants, while others search for insects, fish or other animals. Look for birds among the weeds that grow along the pond's edge, as well as in the water.

Gone fishing

Herons are long-necked, long-legged, long-billed birds adapted for fishing in the shallows. Green herons search for food along the shores of ponds, streams, lakes, and marshes. Like other herons, they have large, slightly webbed feet that allow them to walk in wet places without sinking into the mud. A fishing heron may stand motionless, watching for prey, or stalk with slow, jerky steps. When it spots food, its bill darts out with surprising speed. Green herons eat frogs, fish, and other small aquatic animals.

The great blue heron can be found in ponds, rivers, and lakes, as well as on salt water throughout the United States.

A young green heron takes to the air.

Green herons are common in developed areas as well as remote wetlands throughout the eastern United States, the midwest, and in parts of the southwest and west coast. When the weather turns cold, they leave the northern parts of their range and fly south.

Time in the trees

Green herons spend time in trees as well as in the water. A male will choose a nest site in a tree or bush, and begin piling sticks into it. He then fetches sticks for his mate while she continues to build. The male usually locates the nest near water, a help when it comes time to feed several hungry chicks. Green herons roost in trees at night, and sometimes perch on branches during the day. If you startle one when it is hunting along the shore, it may take off into the trees for safety.

A green heron's niche

"Predator" is one word that describes the green heron, for it hunts other animals to eat. But what distinguishes it from other predators that frequent ponds?

For one thing, its size and manner of hunting affect what it can catch. Like the green heron, the great blue heron fishes in pond shallows, but its much longer legs and bill allow it to fish in slightly deeper water, and to reach food that is farther away from its body. The osprey is a fish eater, but it is certainly not a wader! It flies over the water, dropping down to grab fish with its talons. The predators that share an ecosystem often have different physical adaptations and hunting strategies. This specialization allows them to make use of different food resources.

Plants of the Pond

 Plants are an important part of the pond ecosystem. They release oxygen into the water, and provide animals with food, nest material, and places to hide, rest, and lay eggs.

The white flower pictured here is a water lily in the genus Nymphaea.

Water lilies

Water lily leaves and flowers look like they are just floating on the surface, but they are actually attached to stems. The stems reach all the way to the bottom of the pond. There they connect to a **rhizome**, a special stem that lies buried in the mud. Roots also grow from the rhizome. They anchor the lilies and provide them with water and nutrients.

Water lilies can grow in less than a foot of water. Some species can grow in clear water as deep as fifteen feet. Some lily flowers are quite fragrant, while other species don't have much of a smell.

Look for an aril, the fruit of a water lily, in the shallow water at the edge of a pond.

Water lilies are **perennial** plants: they continue to grow year after year. New plants sprout from seeds that have fallen into the bottom muck. The developing leaves get the energy they need to grow from sunlight that penetrates the water. You won't find water lilies growing out in the middle of very deep ponds and lakes, because not enough light reaches the bottom there.

Look for water lily blossoms in mid to late summer. Like other flowers, water lilies must be **pollinated** if they are to produce seeds. That is, pollen grains from one flower must be transported by insects to another flower. Once pollinated, the flowers close, and the stems coil up, dragging the blossoms underwater. During the weeks that follow, seeds develop in a fruit called the **aril**. Once ripe, the aril breaks off and floats away. As it rots, water lily seeds are released. They sink, and are planted wherever the aril has brought them.

What lives on a lily?

Other plants and animals depend on water lilies. Muskrats eat them, insects lay eggs on them, and small aquatic plants grow from their stems or leaves. Inspect a water lily closely for clues about the community of plants and animals that are associated with it. You may find insects in the lily flower itself. Check the underside of the leaves and the stem carefully for insect or amphibian eggs. You can also collect a little of the green "slime" that often coats large aquatic plants. Study it under a microscope to see if it contains tiny plants and animals.

Duckweed

Duckweeds are the tiny, floating plants in the family *Lemnaceae*.

Sometimes they grow so thickly on the surface of a pond that they form a carpet that looks solid enough to walk on! This carpet is an important source of food for plant-eating ducks, but it can prevent sunlight from reaching other aquatic plants that grow beneath it.

Scoop up some duckweed and look at it. Most species have a green, leaf-like **thallus**, with little roots dangling from it. A duckweed plant usually reproduces by dividing in two, but occasionally you may notice a tiny flower growing out of the thallus. Like other flowering plants, duckweeds can produce seeds that grow into new plants.

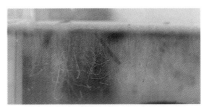

AQUATIC

Snails, worms, insects, and lots of other tiny animals live in ponds. They are aquatic inverte-brates, or water-dwelling animals that do not have backbones. You might not notice them at first, for they are often concealed under rocks and lily pads, or hard to see against the mucky pond bottom. But look carefully. As you get used to looking through the shallow water, you'll begin to notice movements and possible hiding places. If the water is cloudy, deep, or overgrown with algae, you can use a bucket or net to collect some muck. Put it in a pan with some water. As the sediment settles and the water clears, you can see what you have caught. You can also look for animals by sifting through the bottom muck with your fingers, and looking closely at the stones, sticks, and leaves you find in the water.

You might find...

DRAGONFLY AND DAMSELFLY NYMPHS

Dragonflies and damselflies spend the first part of their lives as under-water nymphs. You can find them crawling on aquatic plants or in the silt and decay-ing vegetation on the bottom of a pond or stream. Damselfly nymphs have long, slender bodies with three tail-like gills that allow

them to breathe under water. They move through the water by wriggling their bodies from side to side. Dragonfly nymphs look more sturdy than damselfly nymphs. They have much wider abdomens, which contain a special gill chamber. Both dragonfly and damselfly nymphs eat small aquatic animals.

Eventually, a nymph leaves the water. It crawls up a plant stem or rock, or onto the shore. Its skin splits, and the adult crawls out, unfolding a sur-prisingly long abdomen and wings. When its wings are dry and its body is hard it will fly off in search of food.

Look for adult dragonflies and damselflies flying above fields and ponds, or resting on the plants that grow in the water.

INVERTEBRATES

LEECHES

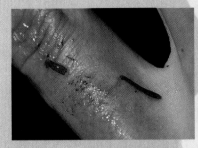

Look for leeches under rocks that you find in the water. Many leeches are nocturnal, and tend to "hide out" during the day. You may also see them swimming through the water, feeding on dead fish, or clinging to a frog or turtle.

Different kinds of leeches have different diets. Some prey on live snails, others are scavengers and feed on dead fish. Many are "blood suckers." Some blood suckers feed on turtles, others on fish or frogs, and a few will take blood from people. Leech bites don't hurt, but most people don't like to see leeches on their skin! If a leech gets on you, you can wait for it to get full and drop off, or you can hurry it along by sprinkling a little salt on it.

PLANARIA

Planaria are tiny flatworms. They avoid light, so look for them under rocks or in the bottom muck. Though they are tiny, you can recognize some species by their triangular heads and two light-colored eyes. Planaria get oxygen by absorbing it through their skin. In places where the water is stagnant and low in oxygen, you may have trouble finding them.

Rearing Aquatic Invertebrates

Most aquatic invertebrates can be brought indoors and studied. You can keep them in shallow pans of water or in aquaria. If the water in your container is deep, make sure to aerate it. If you only keep your sample a few days, you won't have to worry about supplying food. Some of the animals you collected will hunt for others to eat, and some will feed on fresh or decaying vegetation. If you plan to keep your sample for a long time, collect new food regularly, or raise mosquito larvae to feed the insect-eaters.

When you are through with your study, return animals to the same pond you collected them from. Then they will be able to find food, and the temperature and chemistry of the water will suit them.

Looking Under Water

An underwater viewer, such as swim goggles or a diving mask, can help you see what is going on in a pond. It's easy to make your own viewer.

Making a coffee can viewer

A coffee can viewer is the easiest kind to make.

You will need:

- an extra-large juice can or coffee can
- a can opener
- heavy-duty plastic wrap
- duct tape

Instructions:

1. Use the can opener to remove both ends from the can.

One of the animals you can spot with your viewer is a mud snail.

2. Stretch a piece of heavy-duty plastic wrap across one opening.

3. Fasten the plastic wrap securely with duct tape, and you're done!

Take your viewer to a nearby pond, and lower the end with plastic wrap on it into the water. Peer into the open end to see what is below the surface.

A wood and plexiglass viewer

You can make a larger and more durable viewer out of wood and plexiglass.

You will need:

- four wooden boards, 8"x12" or larger
- wood screws
- wood glue
- washers for the screws
- a drill and a screwdriver
- a piece of plexiglass (sized to fit with your boards)
- non-toxic caulk (available at hardware stores)

Instructions:

1. Screw the four boards together to form the sides of a box. Make sure you put glue on the joints first.
2. Fit the plexiglass over the opening at one end, and fasten it in place with screws. Make sure to pre-drill holes in the plexiglass, so it won't crack when you put the screws in place. And use washers between the screwheads and the plexiglass to keep the holes from leaking.
3. Caulk all the joints with non-toxic caulk. Remember to caulk the plexiglass joints as well. When the caulk is dry, your viewer is ready to use.

Experiment with your finished viewer to figure out how to get a clear look at the pond bottom. You may have to put your face down into the box or can to block out reflections.

Pond Turtles

A small painted turtle, Chrysemys picto, *basks on a lily pad.*

 hen you visit a pond, look for turtles basking at the surface. Check protruding rocks, logs, and lily pads, since these are favorite basking spots. When turtles bask, they rest and sun themselves. This warms their bodies, making it easier for them to move, eat, and digest food. Sitting in the sun may also slow the growth of algae and disease organisms on the turtle's shell, and cause leeches that have attached themselves to its skin to drop off.

Snapping turtles

You are likely to see a snapping turtle, *Chelydra serpentina*, if you spend much time exploring ponds, lakes, or marshes in the middle and eastern part of the United States. Sometimes they're even found in salt water along the coast. Watch for them when you're riding in a car in late spring or summer. That's the time female snapping turtles search for places to lay their eggs. Often they choose sunny fields, sand, or gravel banks, or other sites that

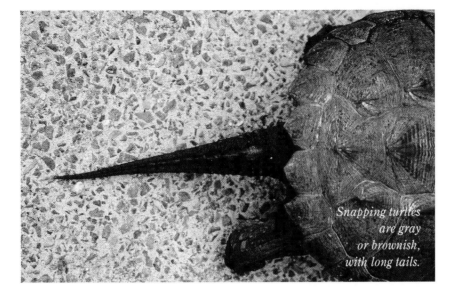

Snapping turtles are gray or brownish, with long tails.

dead animals. During the winter, they often remain active even though the water around them is quite cold. They can also dig themselves into a silty bottom, and spend cold spells buried and inactive.

Painted turtles

The painted turtle, *Chrysemys picta*, has skin marked with patterns of yellow and red, and red designs around the edge of its shell. Painted turtles eat small aquatic animals, decaying carcasses, and aquatic plants. They need to have their heads underwater in order to swallow their food. Female painted turtles tend to grow larger than males. You can recognize adult males by their very long front claws and their long, thick tails. Like snappers, female painted turtles dig nests in the ground to lay their eggs in. The young usually hatch in late summer, tiny, but completely self-sufficient. At four to six years of age, they are old enough to mate and produce young.

bring them close to roads. You can tell snappers from other kinds of turtles by their long tails, long necks, and uniform gray or brownish coloring.

Partly protected

Like all turtles, *Chelydra serpentina* has a bony carapace covering its back, and another shell, the plastron, on its belly. Snapping turtles have small plastrons, which do little to protect the underside of their bodies. They usually avoid danger by swimming

away from it. When cornered, however, they may feel threatened, and hiss or bite. A large snapping turtle can deliver a severe bite, so make sure to observe it from a distance.

Habits

Can you spot the snapper?

Newly hatched snapping turtles have a carapace just an inch long. After hatching, they make their way to a nearby pond, lake, or marsh. Scientists still aren't sure how hatchlings manage to locate these places. Young turtles face many dangers, but those that escape predators and road traffic may live a long time. Snapping turtles nearly fifty years old have been found in the wild.

Snapping turtles spend most of their time in the water. They often sit quietly, partly buried in bottom muck, quickly reaching out their necks to grab fish, frogs, or insects that come close enough to catch. Snapping turtles also eat aquatic plants, ducks, small mammals, and

Snapping turtles have small plastrons, or "belly" shells.

Painted turtles are common in ponds, lakes, and marshes in much of the United States and parts of Canada.

Frogs

You will often see or hear adult frogs when you visit a pond. You may also find young frogs, called tadpoles or pollywogs, swimming in the muddy shallows. Frogs are amphibians, like toads and salamanders. Amphibian eggs lack shells to keep them from drying out, so they must be laid in water or wet soil. Young amphibians usually look quite different from their parents.

Wood frogs lay their eggs in ponds, but spend most of their time in the woods.

Breathe through your skin, swallow with your eyes

Frogs have soft, moist skin covered with mucus. Though they have lungs like we do, they can also absorb oxygen directly through their skin. Some have glands in their skin that secrete chemicals that certain predators find bad-tasting. Frogs eat insects and other small animals they catch. They use their eyes to help them swallow. When they blink, their eyelids push down on their eyes. The eyes, in turn, bulge down into the mouth, and push food towards the throat.

The green frog, Rana clamitans, is common in and around ponds throughout the eastern half of the United States. Green frogs come in different colors. While some are truly green, others are tan, bronze, or brown. Two ridges run down their backs. Green frogs are predators, but they are also prey. Herons, racoons, and snapping turtles are among the animals that eat them.

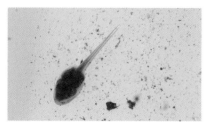

Young frogs are called tadpoles or polliwogs. As they get older, their legs develop.

In danger?

In recent years, some species of frogs, toads, and salamanders have become less common. Why? Our waste products and land-use practices are largely to blame. Amphibians are particular about where they lay their eggs, and many travel considerable distances over land to reach breeding ponds.

Highways and other obstacles may hinder their travel. Amphibians also seem especially sensitive to water, air, and soil pollution. Even in relatively unpolluted areas, our development of wetlands and wooded areas can still reduce the habitat available to them.

MALLARDS

There are more mallards in North America than any other kind of duck, and they are common in some other parts of the world as well. In recent years, mallards, *Anas platyrhynchos,* have expanded both their breeding and wintering ranges. At times they descend on farmland in great numbers and feast on grain. It hardly seems possible that the mallard used to be considered an occasional "wanderer" in the northeast.

This male is molting and has already lost most of his bright head and neck plumage.

58

A new brood

If you visit a pond in the summertime, you may see a female mallard with her ducklings. She might have anywhere from one to ten (or more!) young in her brood. During the day they paddle around, nibbling on aquatic plants.

A female, or hen, mallard usually nests on the ground within a few hundred yards of water. She leads her ducklings to water as soon as they are able to walk and swim, often within twelve hours of hatching! Ducklings and other baby birds that are able to walk and find food soon after they hatch are called precocial.

For the first several weeks of their lives, mallard ducklings are covered with fluffy down. About three weeks later, larger feathers begin to grow in. Within two months this replacement is complete, and the ducklings are ready to fly.

Plumage and molting

Most of the year, male and female mallards look different from one another. Both have a bright blue patch, or speculum, on each wing, but females have mottled brown feathers while males have glossy green heads with a white stripe circling their necks. This is sometimes called their breeding plumage.

In early summer, after they mate, male mallards begin to molt. They lose many feathers, and the new ones that grow in are brown and mottled, much like the females'. Ducks lose all the long flight feathers on their wings during this molt, so they are unable to fly until new ones grow in a month later. Songbirds, gulls, and many other birds molt just a few of these feathers at a time, so they are always able to fly.

Female mallards lose their flight feathers later in the season than males do, after they are through raising their young.

As early as late August, male mallards molt again. New feathers restore their green heads, chestnut breasts, and white neck rings. It is not so easy to tell when the females molt. Their feathers may appear a little duller during their flightless period, but the change is slight.

Notice the different plumage of males and females. Males (top) can be spotted by their glossy green heads and white neck rings, while females have duller, mottled feathers.

Muskrats

uskrats look like little beavers with skinny tails. Like beavers, they are water-dwelling **rodents** (furry mammals with long, gnawing front teeth). Muskrats live in remote areas, but you can find them near towns and cities, too. Look for muskrats in ponds, lakes, streams, and large drainage ditches. Rushes and cattails are favorite foods, so search areas where you notice these plants. You are most likely to see muskrats early in the morning, or as afternoon gives way to evening.

Unlike the beaver, which it resembles, the muskrat has a skinny tail.

Muskrat dens and lodges

Some muskrats build lodges on the water. They make a big pile of mud and plants, then dig out one or more rooms within it. The rooms are above water level, so unless heavy rains flood the pond, the muskrats stay dry inside. Muskrats enter and leave a lodge through tunnels that open underwater. Some muskrats construct smaller shelters in the water to go in when they eat. Not all muskrats build lodges. Some make dens by tunneling into a pond or river bank.

The construction activity of muskrats changes the environment where they live. Sometimes this benefits other animals. Black and Forster's terns often nest on muskrat lodges, and sometimes green herons do as well.

Muskrats are much smaller than beavers, but it can be difficult to estimate the size of an animal that is swimming at a distance from you. Check for the animal's tail: if you can see it, you are looking at a muskrat. Beavers swim with their tails below the surface of the water. Muskrats live throughout much of North America.

Muskrat habits

Muskrats are active all year. In the winter, groups often share a lodge—perhaps it's easier to stay warm in a crowd. During the warmer months, adults are solitary, and tend to avoid each other. Some will defend the territory around their den or lodge from any other muskrats that intrude.

This young muskrat, Ondatra zibethica, *was nibbling grass along the edge of a well-traveled road.*

Muskrats are basically **herbivores**. They eat cattails, water lilies, and many other kinds of plants. In winter they sometimes supplement their diet with small aquatic animals.

A female muskrat, like other female rodents, gives birth to litters of small, furless babies. She may have two or three litters each year, and a litter may include as many as six young! The mother nurses her young, and they grow rapidly. Within a month they are capable of living on their own. They may remain in the mother's lodge for a time, while she raises a new litter in another room, or they may move nearby. Eventually, young muskrats begin building their own small dens or lodges.

Continuing

Once you begin to explore you will discover many fascinating things about these special places. You will also have lots of questions!

You may want to learn more about particular plants and animals that intrigue you, and how to raise them at home, or observe them outdoors.

You might want to identify some of the insects, birds, or trees you notice. You may decide to search for owls or breeding frogs at night, or explore a pond in winter. Sometimes, you will be able to answer your questions on your own. Other times, you will need help.

Many people can help you with your study of ecology. Your parents, friends, and neighbors may know of interesting places you can explore in your neighborhood, and they can help you plan trips to more distant sites. There may also be teachers at your school who are particu-

larly interested in ecology. If you live near a college, university, or research center, call to find out if there are any scientists on staff who can meet with you or answer questions by phone. Check your telephone directory to see if there are museums, nature centers, or wildlife sanctuaries in your area. Such places will be interesting to visit, and will usually have a scientist or educator on staff who can answer questions and suggest projects. Many also offer special programs and classes you may want to attend.

How to Order Specimens and Supplies

Almost all of the specimens and equipment that you can't find or make for yourself can be ordered through the mail or by phone from Carolina Biological Supply Company. If you want to order by phone, you'll need an adult with a credit card. Just give the person on the phone the catalog number listed here next to the price for each item you want. Remember, a shipping and handling charge is added to each purchase.

IN THE EASTERN US
Carolina Biological Supply
2700 York Road
Burlington, NC 27215
Toll free: 1-800-334-5551

IN THE WESTERN US
Carolina Biological Supply
Box 187
Gladstone, OR 97027
Toll free: 1-800-547-1733

Please remember: when you order live specimens, make sure you have everything you need to house and feed them before they arrive. If the specimens are not native to your part of the country, it is very important that you not release them into the wild after studying them—letting them loose in a new environment could disturb the ecological balance in your area. If you're not sure about whether a specimen is native to your area or not, ask the people at Carolina Biological Supply Co. or a biology teacher in your school. If you do have to kill a specimen, freezing it is probably the safest and least painful method.

If you can't find Lichens (pages 12-13) in your area, you can order a set of four live lichen samples for about $11.00 (cat. #15-6400), or get prepared microscope slides of lichens in cross-section for about $3.00 (cat. #97-5200) each. You can order 12 medium-sized live Earthworms (pages 18-19) for about $7.00 (cat. #L 408). Owl Pellets

(pages 20-21) are hard to find on your own, but only cost about $3.00 (cat. #P 1680) each. A Berlese Funnel-kit (pages 24-25) costs about $12.50 (cat. #65-4148). It's probably more fun to make your own Plant Press (pages 30-31), but you can also order a small one for about $12.00 (cat. #66-3045); the blotter paper that goes inside it costs about $5.00 (cat. #66-3046) for 15 sheets. It's not hard to capture Crickets (pages 34-35), but you can order 12 live House Crickets for about $6.00 (cat. #L 715) or a "Little Chirper" Cricket Cage, which comes with a cage, six live crickets, and food, for about $12.00 (cat. #L 717). If there are no ponds near you, you can order live Duckweed samples for about $5.00 (cat. #16-1820). You can order 12 Planaria (pages 50-51) for about $5.00 (cat. #L 210), and three Pond Leeches (pages 50-51) cost about $7.50 (cat. #L 421). Microscopes and binoculars can be very expensive. For field trips, Carolina Biological Supply sells two Folding Pocket Magnifiers, the 5X for about $4.50 (cat. #60-2110) and the 10X for about $7.50 (cat. #60-2112). If you want to get a real microscope, they also sell Panasonic Light Scope, which is a 30X portable microscope with a light and batteries which costs about $35.00 (cat. #59-4900). A high-quality 8x30 pair of binoculars for watching birds and other wildlife costs about $70.00 and comes with a carrying case (cat. #60-2560).

ATTENTION TEACHERS: *Most of the equipment and specimens here are available at quantity discounts for classroom use. In addition to Carolina Biological Supply, these supplies are also available from Science Kit and Boreal Laboratories (1-800-828-7777) and Wards Natural Science Establishment (1-800-962-2660).*

Glossary

adaptation: a physical characteristic or behavior that helps an organism survive.

aerate: to expose to air, or to bubble air into a liquid.

algae: a large group of plants that includes many microscopic species that live on tree bark, and in soil and water. (Some scientists do not classify algae with the plants, but include them in another kingdom.)

altricial: young birds that hatch featherless, and unable to find food for themselves.

amphibian: an animal that lives both on land and in the water.

anterior: near the front.

aquatic: living in water.

aril: the seed-containing fruit of a water lily.

basking: sitting in the sun.

behavior: an action that an organism performs, such as flying, singing, or eating.

botanist: a scientist who studies plants.

breeding plumage: the feathers covering a bird during its breeding season. Some birds look the same all year round, while others have distinct breeding and non-breeding plumages.

brood: a group of young birds that were hatched at the same time.

carapace: in turtles, the shell that covers the back.

carbohydrates: compounds made of carbon, oxygen, and hydrogen. Sugars and starches are carbohydrates.

carnivore: an animal-eater.

castings: soil or sediment swallowed by a worm and excreted at the entrance of its tunnel or burrow.

cavity nester: a bird that builds its nest in a hole in a tree.

clitellum: the light colored "collar"

around the body of an earthworm.

commensalism: a relationship between two organisms that benefits one and does no harm to the other.

community: a group of organisms that live together in the same place.

compost: decaying organic matter.

compound leaves: leaves divided into two or more parts, or leaflets.

conifer: cone-bearing plants, such as pine and spruce trees.

crepuscular: active at dawn and dusk.

decay: rot, or decompose.

deciduous: trees or shrubs that lose their leaves at the end of a growing season.

decomposers: the organisms responsible for decay.

detrivores: animals that eat detritus, or organic matter such as decaying plants and animals.

down: the small, fluffy feathers that cover a baby bird. Adult birds also have down, but it is hidden underneath other feathers.

ecologist: a scientist who studies the relationships between different organisms, or between organisms and their environment.

ecology: the study of living things "at home" in their natural environment. Ecology emphasizes the relationships between organisms and their environment.

ecosystem: all of the living and non-living things in a particular area.

erosion: the wearing away of soil or rock by water or wind.

field marks: distinctive features that can help you distinguish one animal from another.

flatworms: animals in the phylum *Platyhelminthes*.

fledged: acquired the feathers necessary for flight.

flight patterns: characteristic ways of flying (flapping and gliding, swooping, etc.).

fungus: a mushroom, puffball, mold, yeast, or relative. Some scientists consider fungi plants, while others put them in a different kingdom.

habitat: an organism's environment. The place where it naturally lives.

hen: a female duck, chicken, or game bird.

herbarium: a collection of pressed plant specimens.

herbivore: a plant-eater.

hermaphrodites: animals that have both male and female reproductive organs.

home range: the area where an individual animal lives.

humus: a rich layer of soil made of decomposed leaves and other organic matter.

hyphae: the thread-like structures that make up a fungus.

incubate: to sit on eggs in order to keep them warm.

invertebrate: an animal without a backbone.

isopod: one of a group of crustaceans that includes woodlice, sowbugs, and pillbugs.

kingdom: a group of living things. Scientists group all living things into several large divisions, or kingdoms.

labium: a special mouthpart found on dragonflies and damselflies, used for catching prey.

larvae: an early stage in the life cycle of some animals.

leaflets: the parts of a compound leaf.

litter: a spongy layer of soil composed of dead leaves, twigs, dead animals, and other material.

molt: to shed the exoskeleton, skin, or feathers.

niche: a species' role within its community.

nocturnal: active at night.

nymph: the young of some insects.

omnivore: an organism that eats both plants and animals.

ornithologist: a scientist who studies birds.

overwinter: survive the winter.

parasite: an organism that lives in or on other organisms. Parasites typically weaken, and sometimes kill, their hosts.

pellets: packets of fur, bones, and feathers regurgitated by some birds.

perennial: a plant that continues to grow year after year.

petiole: the stalk, or stem, of a leaf.

photosynthesize: to use energy from the sun to make sugar from water and carbon dioxide, as plants do.

plastron: in turtles, the shell that covers the belly.

pollinate: to transfer pollen from one flower to another.

posterior: near the rear.

precocial: young birds that are covered with down and able to hunt for food when they hatch.

predator: a hunting animal.

proboscis: in some leeches, the proboscis is a feeding tube that comes out of the mouth.

pupate: in insects, to change from a larva into a pupa (such as a chrysalis or cocoon).

regurgitate: to spit up, or vomit.

rhizome: an underground plant stem. Unlike roots, rhizomes sometimes have buds and small leaves.

rodent: an animal in the order *Rodentia*, a group of furry, gnawing animals that includes mice and muskrats.

scavenger: an animal that eats dead plants and animals, or garbage.

scutes: the horny plates that form the outer layer of a turtle's shell.

setae: hair-like projections on the bodies of some animals.

snags: dead trees that are still standing.

species: a unique kind of plant or animal.

speculum: the patch of colored feathers on the wings of some ducks.

symbiosis: a relationship between two organisms that live together, benefitting both.

terrestrial: living on land.

thallus: a plant body that is not differentiated into roots, stems, and leaves.